Listen Fi... UPDATED EDITION

Focused Listening Tasks for Real-life Situations

STUDENT BOOK

Jayme Adelson-Goldstein

OXFORD
UNIVERSITY PRESS

Introduction

Listen First provides beginning-level students with communicative listening practice through focused listening tasks. These tasks teach students how to listen, clarify, and respond in typical interactive listening situations. They focus on content areas that reinforce zero-level English instruction. Material is recycled from unit to unit, ensuring student comprehension and progress.

Beginning-level students are often overwhelmed when they try to understand every word they hear. The exercises in *Listen First* get students to focus on specific information and screen out irrelevant material. Passages are short so that students will focus on comprehension rather than memorization. Nonverbal responses, such as circling, checking, and underlining, enable students to demonstrate their listening skills, even at the earliest stage of language learning. Oral production is preceded by numerous passive and active listening exercises and is carefully scaled to the beginner's level.

Each of the ten units of *Listen First* is divided into seven sections:

See It	An overview of content and vocabulary
Choose It	Discrimination activities
Write It	Spelling and/or word dictations
Expand It	Listening tasks featuring new situations in the content area
Apply It	Listening tasks with an emphasis on life skills
Get It Across	Dialogue, intonation, and interactive activities
Check It	Evaluation activities

Listen First Teacher's Book contains prelistening activities that set up lessons, suggested procedures, and follow-up activities. Consult *Listen First* Teacher's Book for a thorough, section-by-section treatment of each unit, answer keys, and a complete audio script.

PRELISTENING

Before students begin working on a unit, they will need some exposure to its context and vocabulary. By starting with prelistening activities, students are able to focus later on specific listening tasks without the additional distraction of processing new vocabulary. Recommended prelistening activities include Total Physical Response (TPR) commands that use realia or visuals, *yes/no* questions with visuals, a preview of the unit dialogue, or a review of related materials students have already learned. Encourage students to listen beyond the interference of words they don't know or have forgotten. This is one of the most valuable lessons a second language listener can learn.

Students acquire the skills needed for communicative listening much more quickly if they feel successful and see progress from one activity to the next. Before listening to the Audio CD, assist students in making predictions about the material as a preview activity.

UNIT PAGES

See It

The first page of each unit introduces students to the content and context of the unit. Vocabulary is presented in a listening passage, and clarification strategies are previewed. In **Section A**, students look and listen only. This may need to be played more than once if students are unfamiliar with the material. In **Sections B** (and **C**), students listen and follow directions—pointing to words, pictures, or numbers structured within a context, such as a classroom or a department store. In addition, students circle, underline, mark with an ✕, and check words, pictures, or numbers in a related context.

These TPR activities are a non-threatening way for students to demonstrate their comprehension. During these activities, assess how much of the content or vocabulary is familiar to students and which items need further review.

Choose It

The second page contains a series of discrimination activities using illustrations or short phrases. Students listen to very short passages and circle, mark with an ✕, match, check, or number the appropriate illustrations based on the information in the listening passage. In doing so, students must focus on a particular aspect of the passage, for example, the part of the body that hurts, and identify the corresponding word or illustration.

Write It

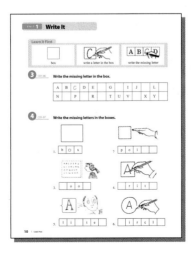

These exercises give students practice in listening for spelling in the first six units, and for focus words in the last four units. The emphasis is always on comprehension, and word boxes are provided when necessary.

The exercises bear a resemblance to more traditional listening exercises, but instead of listening, writing, and then checking, students should be encouraged to write as they listen, with the assurance that they may hear the audio as often as necessary to complete the exercise.

Expand It

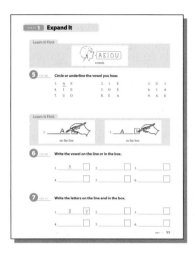

New situations and vocabulary are introduced on the **Expand It** page. Just as in **See It**, previewing new vocabulary will facilitate the listening process. You may choose to work from the text illustrations or with realia to familiarize students with the new ideas. It is not necessary for students to produce the new vocabulary; however, they will need to recognize the new items within the context of the unit.

The tasks are supported by illustrations that set the scene and provide valuable clues to understanding the listening passages. Awareness of visual clues is an essential part of first language listening, and language learners need to remember how to use these cues in second language listening situations. For this reason, picture sequencing and matching activities are often found on the **Expand It** page.

Apply It

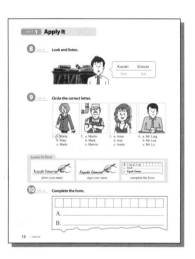

The tasks on this page use vocabulary, clarification strategies, and situations from the previous four pages in a life-skill area, such as taking a phone message, making an appointment, or asking for directions. Students use the familiar techniques of checking, circling, and making an ✕ in tasks that mimic real-life exchanges. The material in **Apply It** sets up the dialogue for the interaction activity in **Get It Across** and provides examples of clarification strategies.

The teacher can expand on this section by providing students with listening experiences outside the classroom. For example, a scavenger hunt involving school personnel, a call to a restaurant or store for directions, or a message left on voice mail will assist students in applying the listening skills learned in class to the real world.

Get It Across

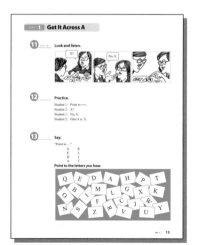

Active, successful listening is the goal of *Listen First*. **Get It Across** provides students with valuable practice in interactive listening. The initial exercise is always a listening passage, emphasizing a particular clarification strategy. The second exercise is the model dialogue, allowing students to see the clarification structure in print.

To help students practice clarification, interference is built into these first two exercises. The first time a question is answered in the dialogue, some information is blacked out with the interference symbol 〜〜. Various noises are used on the Audio CD to suggest interference. In the classroom, students can have fun using their own techniques, such as coughing, mumbling, rubbing their mouths, or anything that prevents the listener from being sure about the answer to the question.

For the third exercise, pages A and B contain complementary information. This is an information gap in which students must obtain information from their partner in order to complete a grid or chart, draw missing objects in a picture, or put locations on a map.

We recommend you have half the class look at page A, and the other half look at page B. Have students listen to the audio for the intonation, clarification, and vocabulary used in the interactive activity. Practice the model dialogue with them, later encouraging them to work on it without you. Pair students, As with Bs, reminding them to look only at their own page when working to complete the information gap. This activity may be done twice, with students pairing up again, taking opposite roles.

Check It

The **Check It** page helps students evaluate their progress in each unit of *Listen First*. The first exercise is similar to those on the **Choose It** page, and the second to exercises in **Apply It**. The last exercise is a TPR activity.

The TPR activity requires students to listen for and demonstrate comprehension in a slightly different way, such as moving, drawing, or filling in a chart. On this last activity, the teacher should encourage students to ask for clarification and may pause and replay the audio as often as necessary. The goal of this activity is for every student to succeed in following directions. This success may come from a variety of sources: students requesting clarification, replaying the Audio CD, students asking other students for clarification, and teacher or student demonstrations.

The evaluation section is not meant to threaten or discourage the student. Encourage students to have fun with the activity.

FOLLOW-UP

The tasks in *Listen First* lend themselves to numerous follow-up activities. *Listen First* Teacher's Book offers a variety of follow-up activities, as well as hints on pairing students, correcting errors, and evaluating performance.

How To Use *Listen First*

1. Preview each page's vocabulary and context with students before playing the Audio CD.

2. Present one task at a time.

3. Review the task type (circling, checking, matching, etc.) with the class on the board.

4. Read or have a student read the directions for the task.

5. Check students' comprehension of the directions.

   - Ask *yes/no* questions: *Are you listening for a number?*
   - Ask *or* questions: *Are you listening for a letter or a number?*
   - Have students restate the focus of the task: *We're listening for the number.*
   - Have students predict the kinds of information they're going to hear: *Phone numbers.*

6. Play the example.

7. Stop the audio and go over the example on the board to check students' accuracy.

   - Have a student do the example and have the class correct it.
   - Have individual students call out their answers and let the class come to a consensus.
   - Circulate around the room and check individual student's work.

8. Play the rest of the exercise, pausing as often as necessary, especially between the first and second items. Repeat Step 7 each time the audio is interrupted.

9. Play the audio again two to four times for students to review and catch missed items. Point out clues in the exercise and write students' suggested answers on the board for discussion.

10. Help students evaluate their accuracy by having the class come to a consensus on the answers. In cases where there is no consensus after four or five listenings, supply the correct answers on the board.

11. Play the audio a final time, enabling students to review the correct answers.

Scope and Sequence

Unit	Listening Focus	Clarification Strategy	Structure
Unit 1 The Alphabet page 8	• Identifying the letters in the alphabet • Discriminating between vowel sounds • First and last names	*or* repetition	present tense
Unit 2 Numbers page 16	• Identifying the numbers 1–10 • Identifying the next number in a sequence • Phone numbers • Identifying mistakes in a phone number	*Excuse me?*	present tense
Unit 3 A Classroom page 24	• Identifying objects in a classroom • Locating objects in space • Giving and following instructions	*Where?*	present tense prepositions
Unit 4 Time / A House page 32	• Identifying the numbers 11–100 • Identifying the rooms in a house • Giving and taking phone messages	rephrasing	present continuous
Unit 5 A Department Store page 40	• Identifying clothing items • Identifying ordinal numbers: 1st, 2nd, 3rd • Giving and asking for prices	*How much?*	adjective placement
Unit 6 A Neighborhood page 48	• Identifying places in a neighborhood • Understanding and using compass directions • Understanding and using street directions • Giving and taking directions to a location	*Wh-* questions	prepositions simple present tense
Unit 7 Health page 56	• Identifying parts of the body • Identifying symptoms of ill health • Making a doctor's appointment	*What?*	simple present tense
Unit 8 The Calendar page 64	• Identifying days and dates • Identifying ordinal numbers • Giving and asking for birthdays	*Wh-* questions	past tense
Unit 9 Employment page 72	• Identifying occupations • Talking about a work schedule • Asking for and giving job skills	*Wh-* questions	*can/can't*
Unit 10 The Weather page 80	• Identifying weather conditions • Identifying seasons • Giving and asking for temperatures	restatement	future tense
page 88	**Alphabet Cards**		
page 92	**Number Cards**		
page 94	**Word List**		

See It

Learn It First

look

listen

A CD1-02 **Look and listen.**

A B C D E F G H I J K L M
N O P Q R S T U V W X Y Z

alphabet

Learn It First

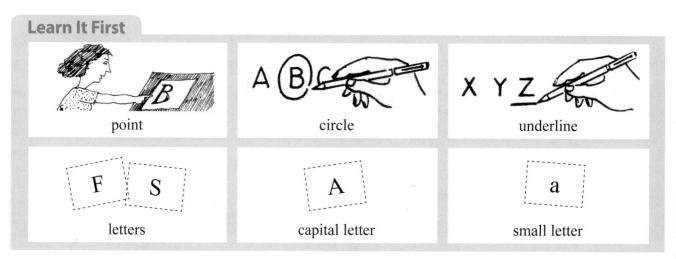

point

circle

underline

F S

letters

A

capital letter

a

small letter

B CD1-03 **Point to the letters.**
Circle or underline the letters.

A B C D E F G H I J K L M
a b c d e f g h i j k l m

N O P Q R S T U V W X Y Z
n o p q r s t u v w x y z

Choose It

1 CD1-04 **Circle the letter.**

1. (C) O	2. V W	3. U V
4. L R	5. F S	6. K Q
7. A H	8. I Y	9. B V
10. G J	11. S X	12. N M

2 CD1-05 **Underline the letter.**

1. L <u>l</u>	2. z Z	3. C c
4. B b	5. E e	6. G j
7. c z	8. k Q	9. C S
10. m w	11. S Z	12. n m

Write It

Learn It First

box

write a letter in the box

write the missing letter

3 CD1-06 **Write the missing letter in the box.**

A	B	C	D	E		G		I	J		L	
N		P		R		T	U	V			X	Y	

4 CD1-07 **Write the missing letters in the boxes.**

1. | b | o | x |

2. 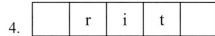 | p | o | i | | |

3. | | o | o | |

4.  | | r | i | t | |

5.  | l | i | | t | e | |

6.  | | i | r | c | l | |

Learn It First

vowels

5 CD1-08 **Circle or underline the vowel you hear.**

1.	<u>A</u>	E	2.	I	E	3.	U	I
4.	I	E	5.	O	E	6.	I	A
7.	U	O	8.	E	A	9.	A	E

Learn It First

1. _____ A

on the line

1. _____ A

in the box

6 CD1-09 **Write the vowel on the line or in the box.**

1. _____ A ☐   2. _____ ☐   3. _____ ☐

4. _____ ☐   5. _____ ☐   6. _____ ☐

7 CD1-10 **Write the letters on the line and in the box.**

1. _____ B ☐V☐   2. _____ ☐   3. _____ ☐

4. _____ ☐   5. _____ ☐   6. _____ ☐

8 CD1-11 **Look and listen.**

Kazuki	Kimura
first	last

9 CD1-12 **Circle the correct letter.**

1. a. Maria
   b. Mary
   c. Marie

2. a. Martin
   b. Mark
   c. Marvin

3. a. Anne
   b. Ana
   c. Annie

4. a. Mr. Ling
   b. Mr. Lee
   c. Mr. Lu

Learn It First

print your name

sign your name

K	i	m	u	r	a					

A. Kazuki
B. *Kozuki Kimura*

complete the form

10 CD1-13 **Complete the form.**

A. _____

B. _____

Get It Across A

11 CD1-14   **Look and listen.**

12   **Practice.**

Student 1:   Point to 〰.
Student 2:   X?
Student 1:   No, S.
Student 2:   Here it is. S.

13   **Say.**

"Point to…."

G   R
E   L
D   J
A   T

Point to the letters you hear.

11 CD1-14 **Look and listen.**

12 **Practice.**

Student 1: Point to ∿∿.
Student 2: X?
Student 1: No, S.
Student 2: Here it is. S.

13 **Point to the letters you hear.**

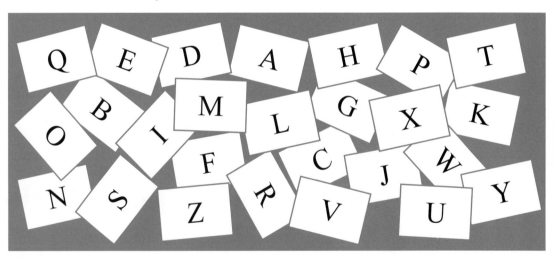

Say.
"Point to…."

Q	V
X	E
S	K
B	I

Check It

14 CD1-15   **Circle or underline the letter.**

1. A E   2. A I   3. A H   4. B V   5. B D

6. B P   7. C S   8. J Y   9. D T   10. C Z

15 CD1-16   **Write the missing names.**

1. _____   2. _____

3. _____ Chang _____   4. _____ Shimizu _____

5. ___ Jane _____   6. _____ Richards _____

16 CD1-17   **Complete the form.**

LOTTERY

A. _____

B. _____

C. _____

A CD1-18　**Look.**

0 1 2 3 4 5
6 7 8 9 10

Learn It First

number

word

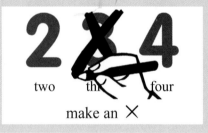

two　three　four

make an ✕

B CD1-19　**Point to the numbers.**
Point to the words.
Make an ✕.

0 1 2 3 4 5

zero　one　two　three　four　five

6 7 8 9 10

six　seven　eight　nine　ten

Choose It

1 <u>CD1-20</u> **Circle the number you hear.**

1. 4 (8) 2   2. 9 8 3   3. 0 10 1
4. 7 5 2   5. 6 9 3   6. 2 7 5

2 <u>CD1-21</u> **Make an ✕ in the correct box.**

1.

a.   b.   c.

2.

a.   b.   c.

3.
   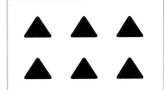   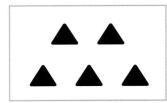

a.   b.   c.

4.
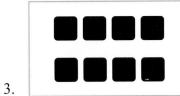   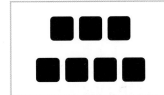   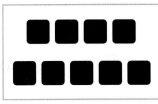

a.   b.   c.

5.
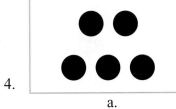      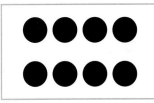

a.   b.   c.

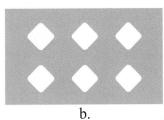

3 CD1-22   **Write the number you hear.**

1. _____3_____   2. _____   3. _____

4. _____   5. _____   6. _____

7. _____   8. _____   9. _____

4 CD1-23   **Write the word.**

THREE.

1. _t_ _h_ _r_ _e_ _e_   2. ____ ____ ____

3. ____ ____ ____ ____ ____   4. ____ ____ ____ ____

5. ____ ____ ____ ____ ____   6. ____ ____ ____

7. ____ ____ ____ ____   8. ____ ____ ____

9. ____ ____ ____   10. ____ ____ ____ ____ ____

Learn It First

5...6...7   ...8

numbers in order   the next number

5 CD1-24   **Circle the next number.**

1. (3)   2   1   2.   6   8   7

3. 7   5   9   4.   4   5   6

5. 1   10   4   6.   8   9   10

7. 3   6   4   8.   6   7   8

9. 5   7   4   10. 10   0   1

6 CD1-25   **Write the next number in the box.**

1. [3]   2. [ ]   3. [ ]

4. [ ]   5. [ ]   6. [ ]

7. [ ]   8. [ ]   9. [ ]

10. [ ]   11. [ ]   12. [ ]

Learn It First

625-7134

phone number

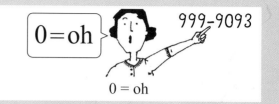

0=oh

999-9093

0 = oh

7 CD1-26 **Listen to the phone numbers.**

671-8997

1.

312-4655

2.

549-2318

3.

990-7324

4.

8 CD1-27 **Write the missing numbers.**

1. 625-_1_134   2. 90____-7439   3. 784-8____42

4. ____96-012____   5. 6____1-____294   6. 99____-____94

Learn It First

559-6902

559-690(3)

a mistake

9 CD1-28 **Circle the mistake.**

1. 5 5 9 - 6 9 0 (3)   2. 4 8 3 - 0 2 0 7   3. 6 8 5 - 0 9 0 1

4. 3 7 2 - 6 5 8 6   5. 4 2 1 - 6 2 3 0   6. 7 5 6 - 2 1 1 3

7. 9 0 8 - 3 6 3 5   8. 5 5 5 - 9 8 9 9   9. 6 2 5 - 6 6 4 9

10 CD1-29 **Look and listen.**

11 **Practice.**

Student 1: 5 7 〰.
Student 2: 5 7 9 ?
Student 1: No, 5 7 10. Show me.
Student 2: 5 7 10.
Student 1: Uh-huh.

12 **Say.**

3 6 9.
1 3 5.
4 8 10.
5 2 7.

Point to the numbers you hear.

10 CD1-29 **Look and listen.**

11 **Practice.**

Student 1: 5 7 〜.
Student 2: 5 7 9?
Student 1: No, 5 7 10. Show me.
Student 2: 5 7 10.
Student 1: Uh-huh.

12 **Point to the numbers you hear.**

Say.

2 4 6.
0 10 9.
3 7 4.
1 8 5.

13 CD1-30 **Circle the correct number.**

1.  5 four

2. zero 1

3. 9 three

4. • 4 ten

14 CD1-31 **Write the next number.**

1. ☐   2. ☐   3. ☐

4. ☐   5. ☐   6. ☐

15 CD1-32 **Circle the phone number you hear.**

1. 555-1211   555-1212   2. 698-9573   689-9573

3. 413-9035   413-0935   4. 327-0965   237-0965

5. 888-8148   888-8158   6. 997-3143   997-4133

16 CD1-33 **Complete the form.**

APPLICATION FORM

1. _____

2. _____

3. _____

A CD2-01 **Look.**

1. a book

2. a pencil

3. paper

4. a clock

5. a student

6. a teacher

7. a pen

8. a picture of a pen

B CD2-02 **Point to the pencils.**

1. next to

2. on

3. under

4. above

5. in

C CD2-03 **Look at the classroom.**
Circle the words you hear.

window

2

board

English

door

student

teacher

paper

book

desk

floor

chair

a classroom

Choose It

1 CD2-04 **Make an ✕ on the correct letter.**

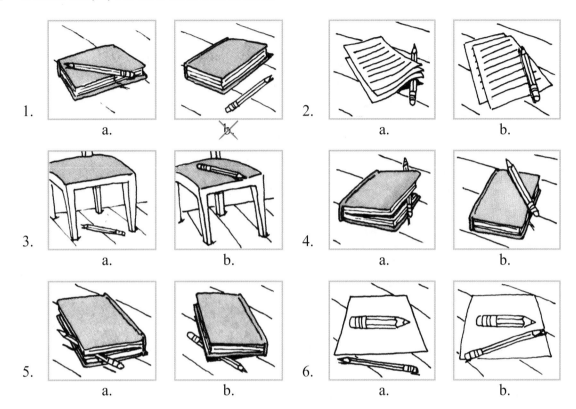

1. a. b.   2. a. b.

3. a. b.   4. a. b.

5. a. b.   6. a. b.

2 CD2-05 **Put the numbers on the picture.**

3 CD2-06   **Write the missing words.**

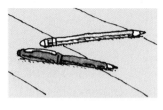

1. The pen is <u>n e x t   t o</u> the pencil.

2. The window is ___ ___ ___ ___ ___ the chair.

3. The pen is ___ ___ ___ ___ ___ the book.

4. The pen is ___ ___ the paper.

4 CD2-07   **Write the words next to the pictures.**

door

Learn It First

on the left

on the right

5 CD2-08 **Look and listen.**

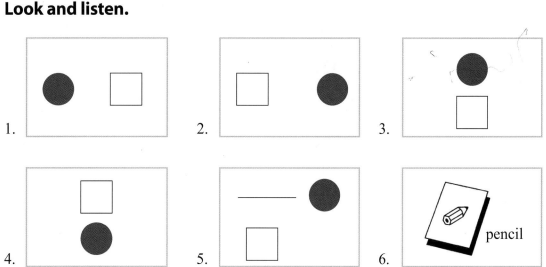

1.   2.   3.

4.   5.   6. pencil

Learn It First

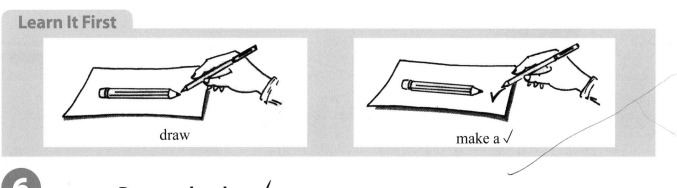

draw

make a ✓

6 CD2-09 **Draw and make a ✓.**

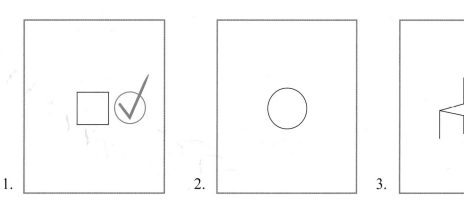

1.   2.   3.

7 CD2-10   **Circle the letter under the correct picture.**

1. a.   b.   2. a.   b.

3. a.   b.   4. a.   b.

8 CD2-11   **Look at the picture. Make a ✓ under the correct answer.**

	above the box	under the box	next to the box, on the left	next to the box, on the right	on the box
1.			✓		
2.					
3.					
4.					
5.					

9 CD2-12 **Look and listen.**

10 **Practice.**

Student 1: Where's the chair?
Student 2: It's next to the board, on the ∼∼∼.
Student 1: On the left or on the right?
Student 2: On the left.

11 **Ask.**

"Where's the…?"

pen

window

5

paper

9 CD2-12 **Look and listen.**

10 **Practice.**

Student 1: Where's the chair?
Student 2: It's next to the board, on the ∿∿.
Student 1: On the left or on the right?
Student 2: On the left.

11 **Ask.**

"Where's the…?
        teacher
        pencil
        1
        book

12  CD2-13   **Circle the letter under the correct picture.**

1.   a.   b.

2.   a.   b.

3. 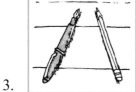 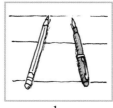 a.   b.

4.   Emma   Emma   a.   b.

5.  Andy   Andy a.   b.

6. 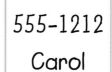 555-1212 Carol   Carol 555-1212 a.   b.

13  CD2-14   **Make a ✓ or an ✕. Draw a line or a circle.**

N	Q	V	K	D
O	J	T	R	U
V	C	Z	H	I
A	I	X	K	B
S	E	F	A	E

14 CD2-15   **Do it.**

Point to your book.

A CD2-16 **Look.**

1. 1:00   2. 1:05   3. 1:15   4. 1:30

B CD2-17 **Look.**
Point to the numbers.

11	12	13	14	15	16	17	18	19
20	21	22	23	24	25	26	27	28	29
30	40	50	60	70	80	90	100		

C CD2-18 **Make an ✕.**

1. at work

2. at home

3. the living room

4. the kitchen

5. the bathroom

6. the bedroom

Choose It

1 CD2-19 **Make a ✓ on the number you hear.**

1. 5   15   50   2. 12   20   22   3. 6   16   60

4. 4   14   40   5. 7   17   70   6. 3   13   30

7. 9   19   90   8. 10   11   100   9. 8   18   80

Learn It First

the correct time

2 CD2-20 **Circle the letter under the correct time.**

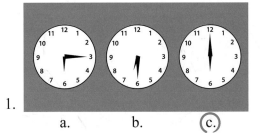

1.
    a.   b.   (c.)

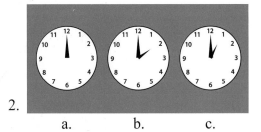

2.
    a.   b.   c.

3.
    a.   b.   c.

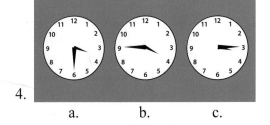

4.
    a.   b.   c.

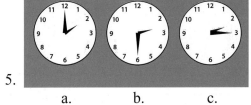

5.
    a.   b.   c.

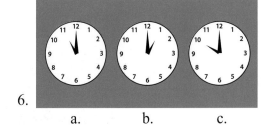

6.
    a.   b.   c.

Learn It First

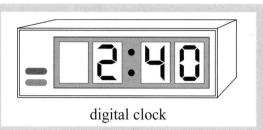

digital clock

3 CD2-21 **Write the missing numbers on the clocks.**

1.

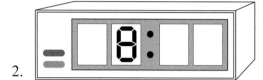

2.

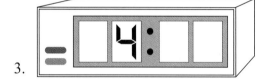

3.

4.

5.

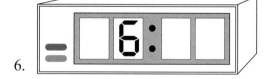

6.

Learn It First

Good morning.
Good afternoon.
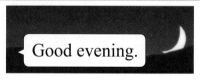
Good evening.

greetings

4 CD2-22 **Write *a.m.* or *p.m.* next to the time.**

1. It's 6:00 ___a.m.___   2. It's 3:00 _____   3. It's 6:00 _____

4. It's 5:00 _____   5. It's 10:45 _____   6. It's 8:30 _____

5 CD2-23 **Write the time on the clocks.**

1.

2.

3.

4.

5.

6.

6 CD2-24 **Listen to the questions and look at the pictures above.**
Circle *yes* or *no*.

1. yes (no)	2. yes no	3. yes no	4. yes no
5. yes no	6. yes no	7. yes no	8. yes no

7 CD2-25 **Write the correct numbers on the pictures.**

Learn It First

leave a message    take a message

8 CD2-26 **Listen to the phone conversations and look at the messages.**

Telephone Message

Time: 4:00

Call: Rick Green
      at home

Number: 550-4321

Telephone Message

Time: 4:30

Call: Ken
      at work

Number: 773-0980

9 CD2-27 **Take the messages.**

Telephone Message

Time: _____

Call: _____

_____

Number: _____

1.

Telephone Message

Time: _____

Call: _____

_____

Number: _____

2.

10 CD2-28   **Look and listen.**

Call David at home, 684-0821.

11   **Practice.**

Student 1:   Hello. Is Ed there?
Student 2:   No, he isn't. May I take a message?
Student 1:   This is David. I'm at home. My number is 684-0821.
Student 2:   Call David at home, 684-0821.
Student 1:   That's right. Thank you. Bye.
Student 2:   Bye.

12   **Listen to your partner.**
Take the message for Kate.

Message for: Kate

Time: _____

Call: _____

at: _____

Phone number: _____

Call your partner. Ask for Arnold.
Leave a message for Arnold.

You are at work.
Your phone number is 956-3121.

10 CD2-28 **Look and listen.**

Call David at home, 684-0821.

11 **Practice.**

Student 1: Hello. Is Ed there?
Student 2: No, he isn't. May I take a message?
Student 1: This is David. I'm at home. My number is 684-0821.
Student 2: Call David at home, 684-0821.
Student 1: That's right. Thank you. Bye.
Student 2: Bye.

12 **Call your partner. Ask for Kate.**
Leave a message for Kate.

You are at home.
Your phone number is 317-1954.

Listen to your partner.
Take the message for Arnold.

Message for: Arnold

Time: _____

Call: _____

at: _____

Phone number: _____

13 CD2-29 **Look at the pictures. Write the correct numbers in the boxes.**

14 CD2-30 **Take the message.**

Telephone Message	Telephone Message
Time: _____	Time: _____
Call: _____	Call: _____
_____	_____
Number: _____	Number: _____
1.	2.

15 CD2-31 **Do it.**

A CD2-32   **Look.**

jacket   shirt   pants   shoes   dress   pantyhose   shoes   hat

sweater   blouse   skirt   socks   shoes

B CD2-33   **Look at the department store.**
Point to the words you hear.

Children's Clothing

Women's Clothing

3rd floor

2nd floor

Men's Clothing

1st floor

department store

C CD2-34   **Look.**
Make a ✓ above the picture.

1.

2.

3.

4.

Choose It

1 CD2-35 **Circle the letter under the correct picture.**

1. 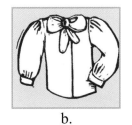    2.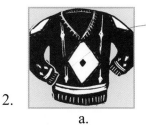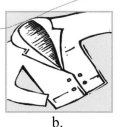
   a.   b.   a.   b.

3.  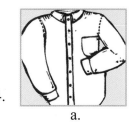   4.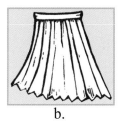
   a.   b.   a.   b.

2 CD2-36 **Make a ✓ next to the words you hear.**

1. ✓ shirt   2. ____ sweater   3. ____ jacket   4. ____ blouse
   ____ dress   ____ pants   ____ shirt   ____ skirt
   ✓ shoes   ____ socks   ____ skirt   ____ pantyhose

3 CD2-37 **Draw a line from the name to the correct picture.**

1. George   2. Hannah   3. Roy   4. Flora

Write It

4 CD2-38 **Write the correct words next to the pictures.**

| jacket | skirt | pants | socks | sweater | dresses |

jacket

5 CD2-39 **Help Simon write his shopping list.**

shopping list

❶ 1 jacket

❷ _____

❸ _____

❹ _____ pairs of _____

❺ _____ pairs of _____

❻ _____ pair of _____

6 CD2-40 **Circle the letter under the correct price.**

1. a. b.   2. a. b.

3. a. b.   4. a. b.

7 CD2-41 **Write the prices on the price tags.**

1. 2.

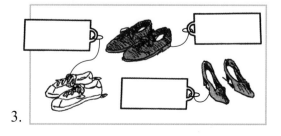 

3. 4.

8 CD2-42 **Make a ✓ in the correct box.**

	1. 		2.		3.	
on sale 50% off						
on sale 25% off	✓					
regular price						

Learn It First

restrooms   furniture   restaurant   offices

9 CD2-43 **Look at the directory and circle the correct answer.**

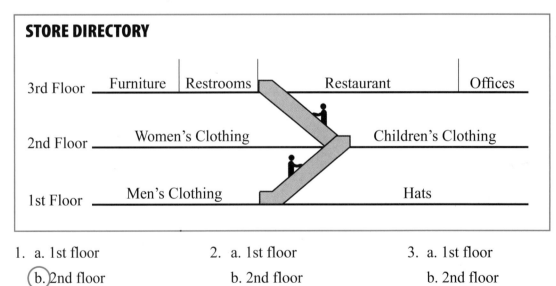

STORE DIRECTORY

3rd Floor — Furniture | Restrooms | Restaurant | Offices

2nd Floor — Women's Clothing | Children's Clothing

1st Floor — Men's Clothing | Hats

1. a. 1st floor
    b. 2nd floor *(circled)*
    c. 3rd floor

2. a. 1st floor
    b. 2nd floor
    c. 3rd floor

3. a. 1st floor
    b. 2nd floor
    c. 3rd floor

4. a. 1st floor
    b. 2nd floor
    c. 3rd floor

5. a. 1st floor
    b. 2nd floor
    c. 3rd floor

6. a. 1st floor
    b. 2nd floor
    c. 3rd floor

10 CD2-44 Look and listen.

How much?

$24.00.

11 Practice.

Student 1: How much is that blouse?
Student 2: Which one?
Student 1: The black one.
Student 2: ∼∼.
Student 1: How much?
Student 2: $24.00.

12 Ask for the missing prices.

$24.00 $19.00 $45.00 $25.00

$22.00 $59.00

$60.00

10 CD2-44 **Look and listen.**

11 **Practice.**

Student 1: How much is that blouse?
Student 2: Which one?
Student 1: The black one.
Student 2: ∿∿.
Student 1: How much?
Student 2: $24.00.

12 **Ask for the missing prices.**

$24.00

$38.00

$22.00

$90.00

$12.00

$40.00

$78.00

13  **Make an ✕, a ✓, or a circle. Write the correct words or numbers.**

1.

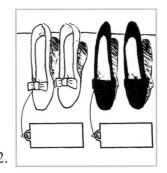

2.

3.

14 CD2-46 **Write the prices on the receipts.**

RECEIPT	
shoes	_____
socks	_____
sweater	_____
pants	_____
shirt	_____
jacket	_____
TOTAL	_____

RECEIPT	
shoes	_____
dress	_____
sweater	_____
blouse	_____
skirt	_____
jacket	_____
TOTAL	_____

15  **Do it.**

A CD2-48 **Look.**

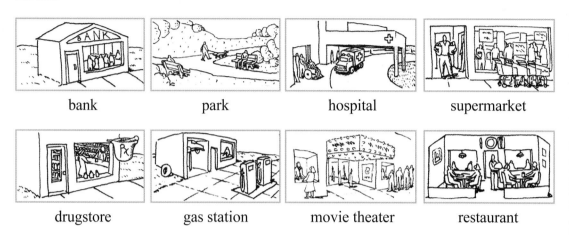

bank   park   hospital   supermarket

drugstore   gas station   movie theater   restaurant

B CD2-49 **Look at the places.
Point to the addresses.**

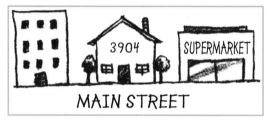

1. between

2. on the corner of

3. around the corner from

4. across from

C CD2-50 **Look and point to the places you hear.**

1 CD2-51 **Write the correct letter on the line.**

1. ___e___

2. _____

3. _____

4. _____

5. _____

6. _____

a. 3930 Green Road
b. 4014 Second Avenue
c. 4012 Second Avenue
d. 3929 Center Street
e. 4041 Center Street
f. 1770 First Avenue

2 CD2-52 **Look at the picture. Circle the correct letter.**

1. a. restaurant
   b. movie theater

2. a. park
   b. apartment building

3. a. bank
   b. school

4. a. gas station
   b. movie theater

5. a. drugstore
   b. movie theater

6. a. bank
   b. park

3 CD2-53 **Write the words you hear.**

1. <u>school</u>

2. _____

3. _____

4. _____

4 CD2-54 **Write the words you hear.**

| ~~next to~~   between   across from   on the corner of   around the corner from |

1. The school is _____<u>next to</u>_____ the park.

2. The restaurant is _____ the drugstore.

3. The gas station is _____ First and Center.

4. The hospital is _____ the supermarket and my house.

5. The supermarket is _____ the park.

Expand It

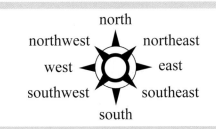

5 CD2-55   **Look and listen.**

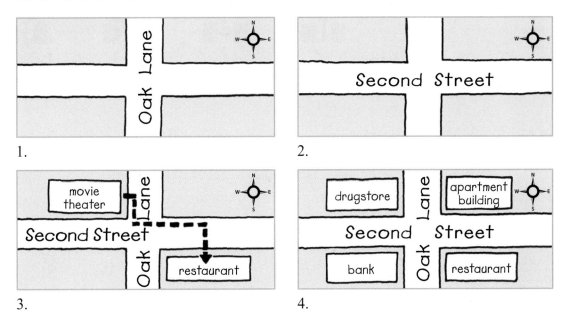

1.

2.

3.

4.

6 CD2-56   **Write the correct numbers on the map.**

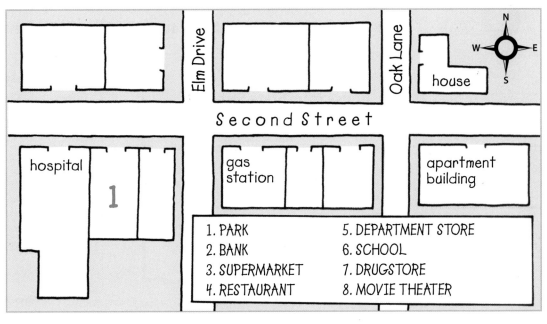

1. PARK   5. DEPARTMENT STORE
2. BANK   6. SCHOOL
3. SUPERMARKET   7. DRUGSTORE
4. RESTAURANT   8. MOVIE THEATER

Apply It

Learn It First

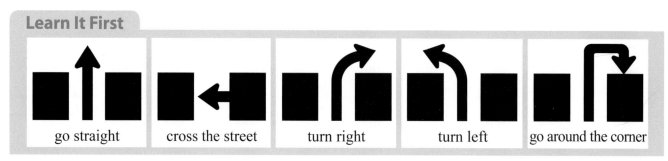

| | go straight | cross the street | turn right | turn left | go around the corner |

7 CD2-57

Make an ✕ under the directions you hear.

	■↑■	■◄■	■↱	↰■	■↱
1.	✕				
2.					
3.					
4.					
5.					

Learn It First

L	R	N	S	E	W	St.	Ave.
left	right	north	south	east	west	street	avenue

abbreviations

8 CD2-58

Use the abbreviations above to write the directions.

1.
Directions to Jean's house from State Street

Go ___N___ on State St.

Turn _____ on Center _____.

Go _____ on Center.

Turn _____ on Pine _____.

2.
Directions to Jean's house from Oak Street and Hill Avenue

Go _____ on Hill _____

to Bay _____.

Turn _____ on Bay.

Go _____ on Bay to Pine.

Address: 5015 Pine _____

Apartment 13

9 CD2-59 **Look and listen.**

Which corner?

The northwest corner.

10 **Practice.**

Student 1: Excuse me, where's the bank from here?
Student 2: Walk north on Pine and cross Second.
It's on the ∿∿ corner.
Student 1: Which corner?
Student 2: The northwest corner.
Student 1: Thanks.

11 **Ask your partner for directions …**

… to the supermarket.
… to the drugstore.
… to the restaurant.
… to the school.

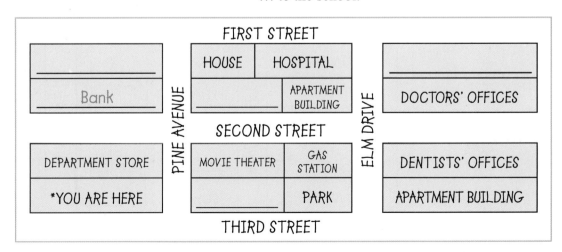

9 CD2-59 **Look and listen.**

10 **Practice.**

Student 1: Excuse me, where's the bank from here?
Student 2: Walk north on Pine and cross Second.
    It's on the ⁓⁓ corner.
Student 1: Which corner?
Student 2: The northwest corner.
Student 1: Thanks.

11 **Ask your partner for directions …**

   … to the park.
   … to the movie theater.
   … to the hospital.
   … to the department store.

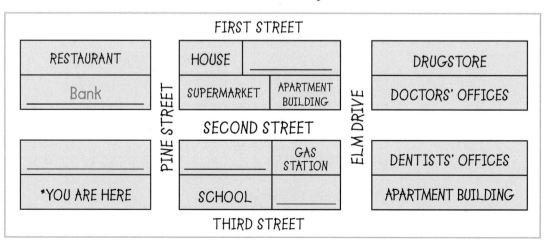

12 CD2-60   **Write the correct addresses on the buildings.**

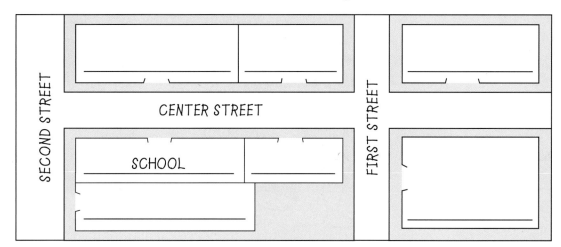

13 CD2-61   **Make a ✓ under the correct location.**

	on the left	across from	around the corner from	between	on the right
1. hospital					
2. school					
3. gas station					
4. restaurant					
5. supermarket					

14 CD2-62   **Do it.**

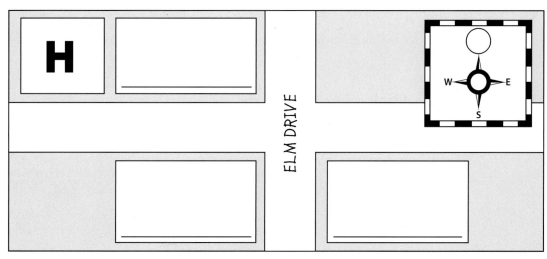

A  CD3-01   **Look.**

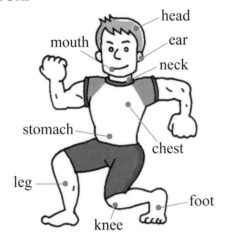

B CD3-02   **Look.**
Point to the pictures.

1. fine   2. sick   3. a cough   4. a cold

5. a fever   6. a sore throat   7. It hurts.

C CD3-03   **Look.**
Make a ✓ under the picture.

1. a backache   2. a stomachache   3. a headache   4. an earache   5. a toothache

1 CD3-04   **Circle the letter under the correct picture.**

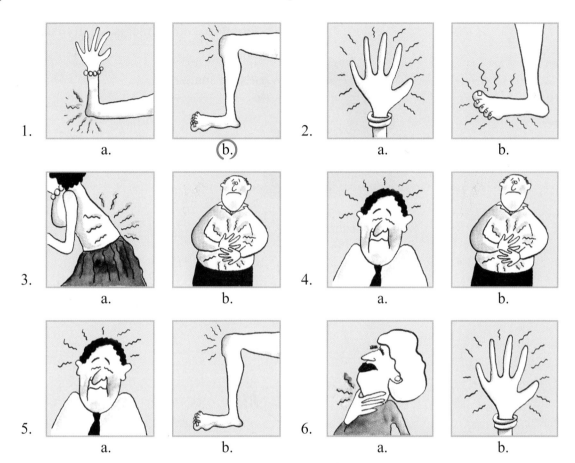

1. a.   (b.)   2. a.   b.

3. a.   b.   4. a.   b.

5. a.   b.   6. a.   b.

2 CD3-05   **Write a number next to the correct part of the body.**

3 CD3-06 **Write the missing letters or words.**

| cold | cough | ~~sore throat~~ | earache | stomachache | backache |

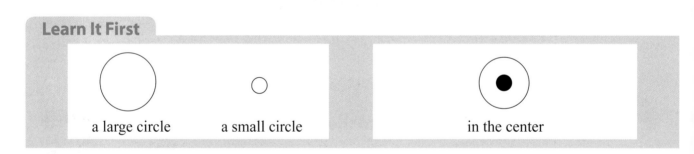

What's the matter?

I have _____ .

1. I have a sore t h r o a t .

2. I have a ____ ____ ____ ____ ache.

3. I have a ____ ____ ____ ____ ____ ____ ____ ache.

4. I have an ____ ____ ____ ache.

5. I have a ____ ____ ____ ____ ____ .

6. I have a ____ ____ ____ ____ .

Learn It First

a large circle   a small circle

in the center

4 CD3-07 **Draw or write what you hear.**

1. _____   2. _____   3. _____

Learn It First

have → need

5 CD3-08 **Look and listen.**

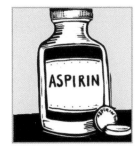   

1. aspirin 2. antacid 3. cough drops 4. a doctor

6 CD3-09 **Write the correct letter on the line.**

1. ___a___ 2. _____ 3. _____ 4. _____

  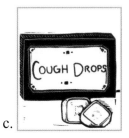 

a. b. c. d.

7 CD3-10 **Circle *yes* or *no*.**

1. a. (yes) no	2. a. yes no	3. a. yes no	4. a. yes no
b. yes no	b. yes no	b. yes no	b. yes no
c. yes no	c. yes no	c. yes no	c. yes no

Learn It First

make an appointment

8 CD3-11 **Make a ✓ under the correct appointment times.**

	9:30	10:45	11:00	11:45	1:45	2:00	4:15
1. Joe Smith						✓	
2. Ling Chan							
3. Jaewon Kim							
4. Michiko Suzuki							
5. Josh Quinn							

Learn It First

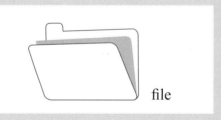

file

9 CD3-12 **Look at the files and circle the correct information.**

1.
Charles Bond
fever / back
9:00 / 9:15

2.
Ken Sato
cough / cold
10:30 / 9:30

3.
Vic Carr
sore throat / arm
9:40 / 9:45

4.
Mika Nakamura
fever / foot
10:15 / 10:50

5.
Joe Green
ear / eye
10:05 / 10:45

10 CD3-13 **Look and listen.**

11 **Practice.**

Student 1: Charles Chan has a 2:00 appointment.
Student 2: What's the matter?
Student 1: He has a ∿∿∿.
Student 2: He has a what?
Student 1: A stomachache.

12 **Ask and answer questions about the appointments.**

Time	Patient	Problem
2:00	Charles Chan	stomachache
2:15	Jane Adams	backache
2:45	Shoko Ikeda	
3:00	Paul Cooper	fever
4:00	Daeyoung Noh	headache
4:15	Bruce Lee	
5:00	Helen Yoshiro	

10 CD3-13   **Look and listen.**

11   **Practice.**

Student 1:   Charles Chan has a 2:00 appointment.
Student 2:   What's the matter?
Student 1:   He has a ∿∿.
Student 2:   He has a what?
Student 1:   A stomachache.

12   **Ask and answer questions about the appointments.**

Time	Patient	Problem
2:00	Charles Chan	stomachache
2:15	Jane Adams	
2:45	Shoko Ikeda	sore throat
3:00	Paul Cooper	
4:00	Daeyoung Noh	
4:15	Bruce Lee	earache
5:00	Helen Yoshiro	cough

13 CD3-14 **Look at the picture. Draw or write the parts of the body.**

14 CD3-15 **Make a ✓ under the problem.**

	headache	backache	stomachache	sore throat	cough	cold
1. Carlos						
2. Flora						
3. Nasim						
4. Bertha						
5. Henry						

15 CD3-16 **Write the correct letter on the line.**

1. _____ 2:15   a. Ms. Sanchez' knee
2. _____ 2:30   b. Mr. Yamamoto's throat
3. _____ 3:00   c. Ms. Johnson's back
4. _____ 3:30   d. Ms. Carson's foot
5. _____ 3:45   e. Toshi Suzuki's shoulder
6. _____ 4:15   f. Mr. Jones' cough

16 CD3-17 **Do it.**

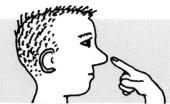

8 The Calendar

See It

A CD3-18 **Look.**

1. a calendar

2. yesterday   today   tomorrow

B CD3-19 **Look at the week.**
Point to the days.

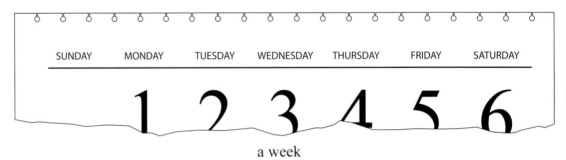

a week

C CD3-20 **Look and point.**
Look and circle.

Su	M	Tu	W	Th	F	Sa
	1	2	3	4	5	6
7	8	9	10	11	12	13
14	15	16	17	18	19	20
21	22	23	24	25	26	27
28	29	30	31			

a month

1 CD3-21   **Make an ✕ in the correct box.**

Su	M	Tu	W	Th	F	Sa
			✕			

1.

Su	M	Tu	W	Th	F	Sa

2.

Su	M	Tu	W	Th	F	Sa

3.

Su	M	Tu	W	Th	F	Sa

4.

Su	M	Tu	W	Th	F	Sa

5.

Su	M	Tu	W	Th	F	Sa

6.

Su	M	Tu	W	Th	F	Sa

7.

Su	M	Tu	W	Th	F	Sa

8.

2 CD3-22   **Circle the correct date.**

Su	M	Tu	W	Th	F	Sa
	1	2	3	4	5	6
⑦	8	9	10	11	12	13
14	15	16	17	18	19	20
21	22	23	24	25	26	27
28	29	30	31			

3 CD3-23   **Write the missing days.**

market	
doctor	
party	
dentist	Monday
bank	
movies	
park	
gym	

4 CD3-24   **Write the missing words.**

yesterday	you	first	Monday	today	your	Tuesday
	work	~~morning~~	Sunday	last		

Good ____morning____ .

   Good morning! Why are _____ wearing _____
pajamas?

Why? Because it's _____ .

   It isn't Sunday. It's _____ .

Are you sure?

   Well, _____ was Sunday. Tomorrow is _____ .

   Yes, _____ is Monday.

Oh no! I'm late for _____ .

   It's not the _____ time.

Good-bye dear!

   And it won't be the _____ .

5 CD3-25 **Look and listen.**

January = **1**	February = **2**	March = **3**	April = **4**
May = **5**	June = **6**	July = **7**	August = **8**
September = **9**	October = **10**	November = **11**	December = **12**

6 CD3-26 **Circle the correct date.**

1. (9/10) 8/9 2. 6/8 8/8 3. 3/12 4/12
4. 1/7 6/1 5. 2/22 4/22 6. 11/5 5/11

7 CD3-27 **Write the dates you hear.**

1. New Year's Day is ___1/1___.

2. Valentine's Day is _____.

3. Earth Day is _____.

4. Halloween is _____.

5. Christmas Day is _____.

6. New Year's Eve is _____.

Apply It

birthday

8 CD3-28 **Make a ✓ under the correct birthday.**

	1/8	2/10	3/4	4/3	8/1	10/2
Martha				✓		
Freddy						
Surijak						
Gloria						
Michiko						

9 CD3-29 **Write the correct letter on the line.**

1. __b__ Helen   a. 12/3/2000
2. _____ Mike   b. 12/3/2003
3. _____ Yasu   c. 12/3/1996
4. _____ Leona   d. 12/3/1998

married

1st child

10 CD3-30 **Write the correct dates on the time line.**

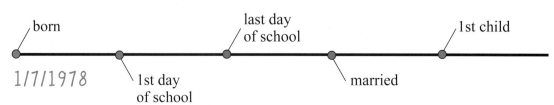

born   last day of school   1st child

1/7/1978   1st day of school   married

11 CD3-31 **Look and listen.**

12 **Practice.**

Student 1: When's Martha's birthday?
Student 2: It's January 〰〰.
Student 1: January what?
Student 2: January 15.

13 **Ask your partner for birthdays …**

… for Lisa.
… for Roger.
… for Myron.
… for Janet.

January						
1	2	3	4	5	6	7
8	9	10	11	12	13	14
15 Martha	16	17	18	19	20	21
22	23	24	25 Frank	26	27	28
29	30	31 Shirley				

June						
		1	2	3	4	5
6	7	8	9	10 Laura	11	12
13	14 Paul	15	16	17	18	19
20	21	22	23	24	25	26
27	28	29	30			

11 CD3-31 **Look and listen.**

12 **Practice.**

Student 1: When's Martha's birthday?
Student 2: It's January 〰.
Student 1: January what?
Student 2: January 15.

13 **Ask your partner for birthdays …**

… for Frank.
… for Paul.
… for Shirley.
… for Laura.

January						
1	2	3	4	5	6	7
8	9	10	11	12	13	14
15 Martha	16	17	18	19	20	21
22	23	24	25	26	27 Lisa	28
29	30	31				

June						
		1	2	3	4	5
6	7 Roger	8	9	10	11	12
13	14	15	16 Myron	17	18	19
20	21	22	23	24	25	26
27	28	29	30 Janet			

14 CD3-32 **Make an ✕ next to the correct day.**

1. ☐ Monday ☐ Sunday 2. ☐ Saturday ☐ Sunday

3. ☐ Tuesday ☐ Thursday 4. ☐ Thursday ☐ Saturday

5. ☐ Friday ☐ Wednesday 6. ☐ Tuesday ☐ Monday

15 CD3-33 **Write the date on the calendar.**

NOVEMBER

Su	M	Tu	W	Th	F	Sa

16 CD3-34 **Circle the correct dates.**

1. October 1 October 31 2. February 14 February 4

3. 12/25 12/5 4. 6/14 7/2

5. 3/12/1996 12/3/1996 6. 9/13 9/30

17 CD3-35 **Do it.**

Personal Information Card

_____

_____

_____

_____

A CD3-36   **Look.**

a computer
programmer

a truck driver

a cook

a salesperson

an office assistant

an accountant

a factory worker

a plumber

B CD3-37   **Look at the employment agency.
Point to the people.**

C CD3-38   **Look.
Look and circle.**

Job Opening	cook
Location	Mario's Pizza
Hours	10:00 a.m. – 6:00 p.m.
Start Date	11/7
Salary	$15.00/hour
Days off	Mondays & Tuesdays

Job Opening	factory worker
Location	NTC Co.
Hours	7:00 a.m. – 3:00 p.m.
Start Date	11/8
Salary	$12.00/hour
Days off	Saturdays & Sundays

1 CD3-39   **Circle the letter under the correct picture.**

1.

    a.   (b.)

2.

    a.   b.

3.

    a.   b.

4.

    a.   b.

5.

    a.   b.

6.

    a.   b.

2 CD3-40   **Write the correct letter on the line.**

1. __d__ cook		a. $25.00/hour
2. _____ factory worker		b. 11/1
3. _____ plumber		c. 8:00 a.m.–5:00 p.m.
4. _____ truck driver		d. 11/6
5. _____ accountant		e. $12.00/hour
6. _____ office assistant		f. 10/30

3 CD3-41 **Write the missing words.**

computer programmer   accountant   plumber   salesperson   ~~office assistant~~

What do those people do?

Excuse me?

What are their jobs?

The woman in the center is an ___office assistant___ .

The man next to her, on the right, is an _____.

The woman next to her, on the left, is a _____.

The woman next to the accountant, on the right, is a _____.

The man next to the plumber is a _____.

Why are they standing in line?

It's their day off. They're all going to the movies.

4 CD3-42 **Write the missing words or numbers on the job board.**

Job	Hours	Salary
cook	10:00 a.m–7:00 p.m.	$15.00/hour
office assistant	8:30 a.m.–5:00 p.m	$12.00/hour
computer programmer		
salesperson	1:30 a.m.–9:30 p.m	

Expand It

5 CD3-43 **Look and listen.**

Can		Can't	
cook		fix things	
drive a car		drive a truck	
make presentations		make spreadsheets	
speak English		speak Japanese	

6 CD3-44 **Make a ✓ when you hear *can* and an ✗ when you hear *can't*.**

	🍳	🧰	📽	🚗	🚚	Hello!	こんにちは
Megumi	✓	✓	✓	✓	✗	✓	✓
Oscar							
Kiyomi							
Bo-han							
Toshi							

Learn It First

What's your job?

Occupation:

occupation = job

part-time/full-time

day shift/night shift

7 CD3-45 **Circle the correct letter.**

1. a. Paul Chan
   b. Paul Chen

2. a. cook
   b. clerk

3. a. full-time
   b. part-time

4. a. night shift
   b. day shift

Learn It First

IVERY   MECHANIC,   TRUCK
, $15/hour, Full-time, $40/hour, Part-time
37-1322   call 342-1919   call 643-

job ad

8 CD3-46 **Read the job ads. Circle the correct letter.**

1.

COOK NEEDED

Mornings
Part-time
$18.00/hour

a.

COOK NEEDED

Afternoons
Part-time
$18.00/hour

b.

2.

FACTORY JOBS

Day shift
Full-time
$12.50/hour

a.

FACTORY JOBS

Night shift
Full-time
$12.50/hour

b.

3.

OFFICE ASSISTANT

Answer emails,
speak English
and Japanese
Full-time

a.

OFFICE ASSISTANT

Answer emails,
speak English
Full-time

b.

4.

DRIVER WANTED

Full-time
$14.00/hour

a.

TRUCK DRIVER WANTED

Full-time
$14.00/hour

b.

Get It Across A

9 **Look and listen.**

10 **Practice.**

Student 1: Tell me about Yu Takeda.
Student 2: He's a cook. He can ⌇⌇⌇ and he can ⌇⌇⌇.
Student 1: He can do what?
Student 2: He can cook Chinese food and he can speak English.

11 **Ask your partner about Anna and Ted.**
Write the information.

Name	Occupation	Skills
Yu Takeda	cook	can: cook Chinese food speak English
Anna Lopez		can:
John Mackie	office assistant	can: make spreadsheets speak French
Ted Darrin		can:
Linda Li	plumber	can: fix sinks speak Chinese

9 CD3-47   **Look and listen.**

10   **Practice.**

Student 1:   Tell me about Yu Takeda.
Student 2:   He's a cook. He can ∿∿ and he can ∿∿.
Student 1:   He can do what?
Student 2:   He can cook Chinese food and he can speak English.

11   **Ask your partner about John and Linda.
Write the information.**

Name	Occupation	Skills
Yu Takeda	cook	can: cook Chinese food speak English
Anna Lopez	accountant	can: use a calculator speak Spanish
John Mackie		can:
Ted Darrin	driver	can: drive a truck speak English
Linda Li		can:

12 CD3-48 **Circle the letter under the correct picture.**

1.
     a.   b.

2.
     a.   b.

3.
     a.   b.

4.
     a.   b.

13 CD3-49 **Circle what the people can do, the salary, and hours they want.**

1.
Naoko Mori	Cook
Chinese food	Italian food
day shift	night shift

2.
Peter Lee	computer programmer
$150.00/hour	$50.00/hour
part-time	full-time

3.
Sue Lanzano	plumber
$20.00/hour	$12.00/hour
part-time	full-time
day shift	night shift

4.
Ray Bean	office assistant
write reports	make spreadsheets
part-time	full-time
day shift	night shift

14 CD3-50 **Do it.**

Job Form

1. _____ _____
2. part-time full-time
3. day shift night shift
4. a. _____ b. _____
5. _____

A CD3-51   **Look.**

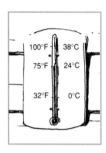    

1. a thermometer 2. cold   3. cool   4. warm   5. hot

B CD3-52   **Look at the weather.**
Point to the cities.

1. sunny   2. cloudy   3. windy   4. smoggy

5. foggy   6. raining   7. snowing

C CD3-53   **Point.**
Circle.

1. beach 65°F   2. city 78°F   3. desert 98°F

4. valley 45°F   5. mountains 29°F

1 CD3-54   **Circle the correct letter.**

1.   (a.)   b.
2.   a.   b.

3.   a.   b.
4.   a.   b.

5.   a.   b.
6.   a.   b.

2 CD3-55   **Make a ✓ next to the correct word.**

1.  sunny
    ____ cloudy
    ____ foggy

2. ____ sunny
    ____ cloudy
    ____ foggy

3. ____ raining
    ____ cloudy
    ____ foggy

4. ____ foggy
    ____ cloudy
    ____ smoggy

5. ____ windy
    ____ raining
    ____ foggy

6. ____ cloudy
    ____ foggy
    ____ raining

3 CD3-56   **Write the missing words.**

cool   ~~warm~~   cloudy   sunny   smoggy   foggy   windy

Here's our weather report for the week.

Today will be _____*warm*_____ and about 70°.

Sunday will be _____ and 90°.

Monday will be _____ and 92°.

Tuesday will be _____ and 75°.

Wednesday will be _____ and 70°.

Thursday will be _____ and 65°.

Friday will be _____, with rain in the afternoon and temperatures in the 60's.

4 CD3-57   **Write the high and low temperatures.**

	 city	beach	valley	mountains	desert
High	78°				
Low	45°				

5 CD3-58 **Look and listen.**

spri   fall   winter

6 CD3-59 **Write th**   se   Buddy

Learn It First

   don't like

7 CD3-60 **Make a ✓ w**
Make an ✗

	spring	summer	fall	winter
Lily	✓	✓	✓	✗
Gary				
Jordan				
Tanya				

8 CD3-61 **Listen and look.**

raincoat · sunglasses · sweater · scarf · umbrella · coat · boots · jacket · hat · bathing suit

9 CD3-62 **Circle the correct letter.**

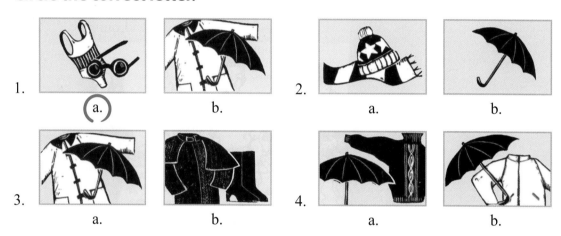

1. a. b. 2. a. b.

3. a. b. 4. a. b.

Learn It First

airport closed

road closed

10 CD3-63 **Make an ✕ under the airports and roads that are closed.**

City	✈	101	5	10	95
1. Los Angeles	✕			✕	
2. New York					
3. Miami					
4. Chicago					
5. San Francisco					

11 CD3-64 **Look and listen.**

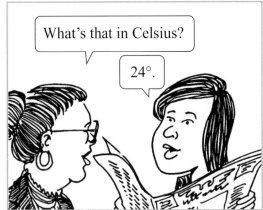

12 **Practice.**

Student 1: What's the weather in Los Angeles?
Student 2: It's sunny and warm.
Student 1: What's the temperature?
Student 2: It's 75° Fahrenheit.
Student 1: What's that in Celsius?
Student 2: 24°.

13 **Ask your partner for the missing information.**

City	Weather	Temperature	
		Fahrenheit	Celsius
Los Angeles	sunny and warm .	75°	24°
New York	sunny and cold	45°	7°
Honolulu		90°	32°
San Francisco	foggy and cool		
Tokyo	cloudy and warm		
San Salvador		84°	29°
Mexico City		90°	32°

11 CD3-64   **Look and listen.**

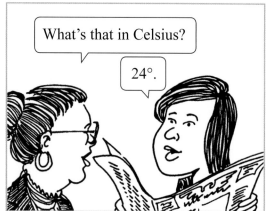

12   **Practice.**

Student 1: What's the weather in Los Angeles?
Student 2: It's sunny and warm.
Student 1: What's the temperature?
Student 2: It's 75° Fahrenheit.
Student 1: What's that in Celsius?
Student 2: 24°.

13   **Ask your partner for the missing information.**

City	Weather	Temperature	
		Fahrenheit	Celsius
Los Angeles	sunny and warm	75°	24°
New York		45°	7°
Honolulu	cloudy and hot		
San Francisco		63°	17°
Tokyo		75°	24°
San Salvador	cloudy and warm		
Mexico City	sunny and hot	90°	32°

14 CD3-65 **Circle the correct letters.**

1. a. hot
    b. warm
    c. cool
    d. cold

2. a. hot
    b. warm
    c. cool
    d. cold

3. a. windy
    b. smoggy
    c. raining
    d. cloudy

4. a. smoggy
    b. foggy
    c. sunny
    d. cloudy

5. a. hot and smoggy
    b. warm and cloudy
    c. cool and windy
    d. cold and raining

15 CD3-66 **Write the correct letter on the line.**

_____ 1. Monday

_____ 2. Tuesday

_____ 3. Wednesday

_____ 4. Thursday

_____ 5. Friday

_____ 6. Saturday

_____ 7. Sunday

a. 90°F/32°C

b. 45°F/7°C

c. 63°F/17°C

d. 50°F/10°C

e. 111°F/44°C

f. 84°F/29°C

g. 75°F/24°C

16 CD3-67 **Do it.**

A	B	C
D	E	F
G	H	I
J	K	L
M	N	O
P	Q	R

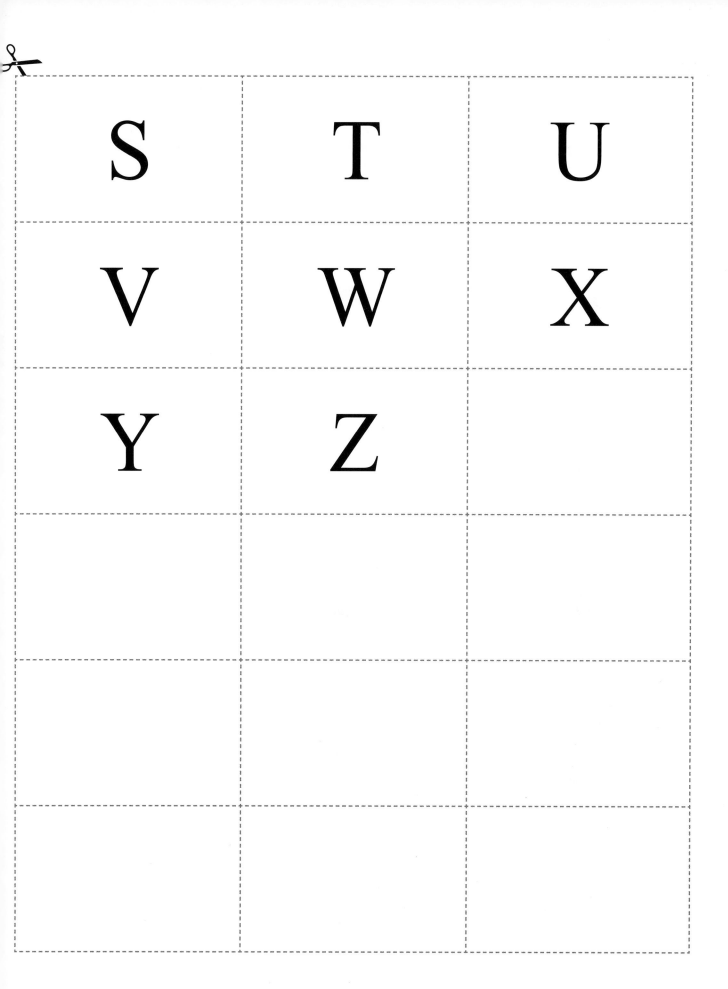

S	T	U
V	W	X
Y	Z	

Alphabet Cards |

a	b	c
d	e	f
g	h	i
j	k	l
m	n	o
p	q	r

s	t	u
v	w	x
y	z	

Alphabet Cards |

1	2	3
4	5	6
7	8	9
10		

20	30	40
50	60	70
80	90	100

Listen First Word List

This word list contains all the 'Learn It First' vocabulary. Words in italics are other key vocabulary introduced within the unit.

Unit 1

box
capital letter
circle
complete the form
in the box
letters
listen
look
on the line
point
print your name
sign your name
small letter
underline
vowels
write a letter in the box
write the missing letter

Unit 2

0 = oh
eight
five
four
make an ✕
a mistake
the next number
nine
number
numbers in order

one
phone number
seven
six
ten
three
two
word
zero

Unit 3

above
board
book
chair
a clock
desk
door
draw
floor
in
make a check (✓)
next to
on
on the left
on the right
paper
a pen
a pencil
a picture of a pen

student
teacher
under
window

Unit 4

at home
at work
the bathroom
the bedroom
the correct time
digital clock
Good afternoon.
Good evening.
Good morning.
greetings
the kitchen
leave a message
the living room
take a message

Unit 5

1st floor
2nd floor
3rd floor
blouse
children's clothing
dress

furniture

hat

jacket

men's clothing

offices

pants

pantyhose

restaurant

restrooms

shirt

shoes

skirt

socks

sweater

women's clothing

Unit 6

abbreviations

across from

around the corner from

Ave. = avenue

bank

between

cross the street

drugstore

E = east

east

gas station

go around the corner

go straight

hospital

L = left

movie theatre

N = north

northeast

northwest

on the corner of

park

R = right

restaurant

S = south

southeast

southwest

St. = street

supermarket

turn left

turn right

W = west

Unit 7

arm

a backache

chest

chin

a cold

a cough

ear

an earache

eye

a fever

fine

finger

foot

hair

hand

have

head

a headache

in the center

It hurts.

knee

a large circle

leg

make an appointment

mouth

neck

need

nose

sick

a small circle

a sore throat

stomach

a stomachache

a toothache

Unit 8

1st child

April

August

birthday

a calendar

December

February

Friday

January

July

June

March

married

May

Monday

a month

November

October

Saturday

September

Sunday

Thursday

today

tomorrow

Tuesday

Wednesday

a week

yesterday

Unit 9

an accountant

a computer programmer

cook

day shift

drive a car

drive a truck

a factory worker

fix things

full-time

job

job ad

make presentations

make spreadsheets

night shift

occupation

an office assistant

part-time

a plumber

a salesperson

speak English

speak Japanese

Unit 10

airport closed

bathing suit

beach

boots

city

cloudy

coat

cold

cool

desert

don't like

fall

foggy

hat

hot

jacket

like

mountains

raincoat

raining

road closed

scarf

smoggy

snowing

spring

summer

sunglasses

sunny

sweater

a thermometer

umbrella

valley

warm

windy

winter